IN PURSUIT
OF BEAUTY

IN PURSUIT OF BEAUTY

THE INTERIORS OF TIMOTHY WHEALON

RIZZOLI
NEW YORK

New York Paris London Milan

To my grandmother,
Beatrice Marie Moquin,
who taught me by
example that beauty
lies in simplicity

CONTENTS

INTRODUCTION

not with the intention of becoming an interior designer. My parents had told me that "art should be an avocation not a career." When I graduated from Kenyon College, my first stop was Wall Street. I was accepted into a management-training program at one of New York's large commercial banks, where I spent six months studying the intricacies of accounting and corporate finance before becoming a lending officer in private banking.

Fortunately, New York's myriad galleries and museums offered welcome relief from the world of corporate finance, allowing me to indulge my passion for the decorative arts. I went so far as taking a weekend job at Stair & Company on Madison Avenue, one of the preeminent English antiques dealers in New York at the time. I realized that I had more interest in furniture than finance, so I resigned to spend a year in London completing the Works of Art course at the Sotheby's Institute of Art. Our program had weekly tutorials at the National Gallery, the Wallace Collection, and the Victoria and Albert Museum. I studied at many of the great English country houses such as Syon, Hatfield House, Spencer House, Chiswick House, Holkham Hall, and Houghton Hall. I was inspired by my visits to the V&A and these great houses, where I savored every aspect of their history and the connection between the decorative arts and the architecture that contained them.

London was the ideal classroom—the embodiment of the classical aesthetic I was rapidly embracing. Having spent my junior year of college abroad at the University of Edinburgh studying art history and English literature, I had fallen in love with the neoclassical Georgian architecture of Robert Adam and the beautiful crescents in the New Town. I spent more than a few weekends in Paris, where I passed the days at the Centre Pompidou and soaked up the café society and everything thing else the City of Light had to offer.

I returned to New York for the Sotheby's management training program, where I had monthly rotations within almost every department, giving me a comprehensive view of the inner workings of both the business and curatorial sides of the auction house. This was a life-changing experience. I was able to view objects up close, handle them, and observe the experts cataloguing and evaluating their condition—a very different experience from my years of studying art in an academic setting. It was a critical moment in the development of my own eye.

Another great opportunity to examine art up close came when I was hired to catalogue the decorative arts collection of Saul and Gayfryd Steinberg, who lived in the thirty-four-room triplex penthouse at 740 Park Avenue that had belonged to John D. Rockefeller. The late Mark Hampton had decorated the apartment for the Steinbergs, and from my perspective it was a fascinating, less patinated American version of the great country houses I had visited in England. The difference was that these impressive rooms were virtually floating on top of Manhattan. I spent one day a week cataloguing objects room by room, soaking up every detail of the finishes, passementerie, and rare art, antiques, and porcelain.

A fortuitous encounter led to my first job as an interior designer. At a charity event, I sat next to a woman from Aspen who had just purchased an apartment on Fifth Avenue. I was intrigued when she told me she collected the paintings of Joan Mitchell, who is one of my all-time favorite artists. When she learned that I had trained at Sotheby's and loved Mitchell's abstract expressionist canvases, she asked me to assist her with the renovation and decoration of her new apartment. Soon after, I met the media executive William Reilly, who had just bought a town house on Sutton Square overlooking the East River. He hired me to purchase all the art and antiques for the town house as well as consult on the architectural finishes, windows, and hardware. Thus Timothy Whealon, Inc. was launched out of my apartment on East 69th Street.

The most pivotal moment in my career came when a client I'd met during my studies in England purchased a decrepit Grade II–listed, late-Georgian house in London. He entrusted me with all aspects of its transformation—from hiring the architect for the restoration to the decoration and purchase of the art and antiques. While in the midst of this massive project, I knew I had found my true calling. The project meant I would be returning to London, so I sublet a flat in Chelsea belonging to India Hicks, who had moved to the Bahamas by that time. I often worked from the desk in the living room, where she kept the most beautiful gilt-framed watercolors painted by her father, the internationally renowned decorator David Hicks. They were so intimate and poetic. I was already a fan of his work, and the watercolors were a daily reminder of his artistry and legacy. I began to study Hicks's work by delving into his books and

visiting the David Hicks store in Paris. The way he reinterpreted classicism and the decoration of English country houses had an important influence on me.

In retrospect, I see that my childhood on the north shore of Milwaukee prepared me for my profession in many ways. I was an artistic child who collected butterflies, stamps, and coins. I always had my own garden and loved watching plants and flowers take root and bloom. Both architect David Adler and his sister, the designer Frances Elkins, grew up in Milwaukee, and one of my favorite buildings was an art museum called Villa Terrace, which Adler had built as a private residence in the 1920s. My mother had an interest in houses and was always redecorating, so I'd accompany her to auctions and estate sales. When I was twelve, I bought my first pair of silver Sheffield candlesticks and a Georgian chair, and I've been collecting ever since.

Growing up on Lake Michigan, I developed an appreciation for wide, open spaces, natural scenery, and the reflection of light on water. Today, I begin every project by looking out the

ABOVE: Baroque tapestry cartoons flank the walls of my first apartment on the Upper East Side. PREVIOUS PAGE: Elle Décor photographed me at home in 2000.

window, as the space beyond is just as important as the room I am creating and often informs my design decisions. Whether the view is of rooftops and water towers or rolling hills and specimen trees, I am influenced by the outdoors, nature, and the play of light within a room.

More often than not, travel influences my work. Whether I am in Italy, South Africa, Ireland, Chicago, or Los Angeles, I buy objects that speak to me, often without knowing where I will use them. I love the mix of high and low, so I am just as happy shopping at flea markets and regional antique fairs such as Brimfield in Massachusetts as I am at the more upscale antique stores in Paris on the left bank and rue du Faubourg St-Honoré. But no place is more magical to me than Istanbul, where I frequent the little shops in the Grand Bazaar in search of rugs, tiles, and textiles. With its mix of Byzantine, Christian, and Muslim influences, the city itself is indicative of the way I combine diverse objects and artworks in my projects.

I am always inspired by visiting galleries and museums when I travel, and over the years I have developed a small collection of works on paper and photography. I vividly remember the first drawing I ever bought from the gallerist Sandra Gering: a conceptual piece that represents the movement of a New York City subway by William Anastasi. The artist Giuseppe Penone is a favorite of mine, because of the tactile beauty of his works on paper as well as the powerful message behind the imprint of pen and ink. I love the work of Ellsworth Kelly and Agnes Martin, who reduce objects to bare, powerful elements that I find poignant and poetic.

Although I never worked for another interior designer, there are many I admire. Like many of my peers, I've read every book that Billy Baldwin wrote. David Hicks and Albert Hadley both had a fresh, modern sensibility that was grounded in classicism, and I consider them two of my greatest teachers. I respect Jed Johnson, Stephen Sills, and Rose Tarlow for their restraint and appreciation for quality and craftsmanship; I admire Jacques Grange for the artful mix in his interiors and Victoria Hagan for the way she thoughtfully and artfully edits hers. Bunny Williams knows more about comfort and luxury than anyone, and she carries the torch for Parish Hadley, whose rooms I have studied in detail. My good friend Marjorie Shushan taught me about the business of interior design, and my friend Martyn Lawrence Bullard taught me that color and laughter will enliven any interior project. And my dear friend, the famed London decorator David Collins, who sadly passed away in the summer of 2013, taught me that the quest for the most perfect shade of blue, the most flattering lighting, and an acute sensitivity to architecture and space yield results that imbue places with beauty and soul.

My style, however, is my own. With a European's reverence for history, a New Yorker's need to stay on the cutting edge, and a Midwesterner's sense of practicality, I strive to create rooms that have a sense of harmony and comfort—that are airy, edited, rooted in the past, and informed by the present. If I had to choose one word as my design mantra it would be purity—my interiors, whether grand or casual, have a purity at their base that conveys a feeling of openness, space, and light. With a love for both classicism and modernity, I hope to create interiors that stand the test of time.

OPPOSITE: My Fifth Avenue apartment had a Swedish-inspired palette. A suite of Agnes Martin lithographs hangs above a Jansen-style sofa and a French bronze side table.

GRAMERCY PARK
PENTHOUSE

A penthouse in a prewar New York City

building is the best sort of compromise, if you can call it that. Often built as maid's quarters, these apartments tend to be small—but the terraces, light, and views are priceless. My current apartment in a 1928 building by master architect Emery Roth has a terrace overlooking both the historic Met Life clock tower and New York Life Building. Simplicity was my mantra as I planned the gut renovation and decoration with the goals of keeping the focus on the views through the handsome casement windows and making sure I had enough uninterrupted wall space for my art.

I wanted the apartment to be a light-filled refuge that took advantage of its northern exposure. The walls are painted in a Ralph Lauren gray with a chalky finish to complement and contrast with the hand-rubbed, high-gloss lacquer cabinetry that has a reflective quality. I replaced the floors with a cerused walnut in a chevron pattern, which adds an old-world element. The Billy Baldwin–inspired sofa is covered in a tactile greige Belgian linen; I designed it in elevation with the windows so it wouldn't detract from the views. I kept all the furniture in the living room low-slung, which adds to the downtown, casual vibe of the apartment.

My collection of contemporary photographs, works on paper, and Indian miniature paintings lines a wall of the living room and defines the character of the bedroom. The black and white honeycomb-patterned linen I used for my bed has just enough pizzazz to enliven the room without interfering with the art. Both the bathroom and kitchen incorporate the same veined Calacatta marble, which gives the apartment a cohesiveness.

The terrace is what sold me on the apartment. I redid the awning in a black and white stripe that has a *Breakfast at Tiffany's* feel and a timeless Manhattan style. The furniture, made by an Australian company called Harbour Outdoor, has sleek lines that complement the cedar screen and boxwood hedge that define the outdoor space. I searched long and hard to find the right clay planters from Belgium as well as the all-weather gray and white fabric with the texture and classic chic of a Chanel suit. The apartment is a peaceful oasis in the midst of the city.

OPPOSITE: The custom white lacquer cabinets and marble counters in the open kitchen characterize my bright, airy apartment. The new chevron floors throughout are from Walking on Wood, London. PREVIOUS PAGES: The Billy Baldwin–style sectional sofa upholstered in Belgian gray linen is low slung so it does not disrupt the expansive views. Geometric throw pillows in a David Hicks fabric are mixed in with needlepoint Jonathan Adler pillows. The linen-wrapped coffee table sits on a black and natural abaca rug by Merida. OPENING PAGE: Hung on walls painted a chalky Ralph Lauren gray, an industrial mirror reflects the apartment's glorious light and the historic buildings beyond.

My work has a sense of timelessness, but it's also a bit modern—a little bit old and a little bit new. I aim for a clean, fresh classicism that has the openness of an Agnes Martin painting.

The most important aspect of this renovation and decoration was creating a backdrop for my collection of quiet photographs and works on paper, as well as the more colorful, graphic prints of Ellsworth Kelly, one of my favorite artists. PREVIOUS PAGE, LEFT: The living room chairs are from the historic collaboration between Pierre Jeanneret and Le Corbusier at Chandigarh, and the landscape painting is by Brazilian artist Lucas Arruda. PREVIOUS PAGE, RIGHT: The combination of contemporary art with a Victorian mahogany two-part brass-mounted campaign chest and antique garden bust reflects my varied tastes and my interest in the juxtaposition between contemporary and antique elements.

The marble in the bathroom is the same stone used in the kitchen, which ties
the apartment together. The showerhead is by Hansgrohe and the mixer
is by Davinci Collection. OPPOSITE: An Inez and Vinoodh photograph hangs
over the bed upholstered in a black and white honeycomb-patterned linen.
A side chair from Restoration Hardware is upholstered in a Marimekko fabric.

The black and white striped awning is classic for a Manhattan penthouse. The furniture from Harbour Outdoor has cushions and pillows in Mariaflora fabric. The boxwood planters are from Atelier Vierkant in Belgium. Edmund Hollander consulted with me on the terrace renovation. OPPOSITE: The view of the Metropolitan Life clock tower is breathtaking day or night. The outdoor room has a custom cedar bench, which serves as a screen along with the boxwood hedge.

CARNEGIE HILL TOWN HOUSE

Eclectic is an overused interior design buzzword, but it's the best description for this six-story town house on Manhattan's Upper East Side. There is a balanced mix of contemporary art, ethnic objects, fine antiques, and custom details. The look is uptown bohemian: *decorated* but with an *undecorated* attitude.

In a town house, the stair landings are crucial spaces, establishing segues between rooms and floors. The first-floor landing beautifully links the living and dining rooms, with a French 1940s chandelier, Moroccan brass sconces, nineteenth-century Chinese carved stools, and an antique Turkish rug. The custom upholstered bench provides extra seating for cocktail parties. Candida Höfer's photograph of a gallery at the Museo Archeologico Nazionale Venezia opens up the windowless space; I used this moment to create a room within a room.

The living room's subtly waxed Venetian walls—which read as lavender, gray, or blue, depending on the time of day—are an ideal backdrop for furnishings that look as though they were collected during a European Grand Tour. The dining room is more dramatic, since it is primarily reserved for special occasions. I hung the clients' edgy cutouts by the contemporary artist Kara Walker over a Parsons-style table I designed with a herringbone faux-ivory finish. The result is ethereal and sophisticated but unpretentious.

The master bedroom is restrained and restful. The soft blue-gray palette creates the feeling of a luxurious hotel suite with the addition of personality and patina. I chose a dove gray and cream printed David Hicks linen for the curtains and bed, quilting the fabric on the headboard to give the room more texture and dimension. As in other parts of the house, the art adds a modern edge to what otherwise might be considered a traditional room.

One of the benefits of town house living is having both a ground-floor garden and a top-floor terrace, and I approached both as indoor/outdoor rooms. The lower-level patio is off the daughter's bedroom, so I kept it lighthearted with a vintage set of 1960s Sculptura wire chairs and a teak lattice fence covered by climbing hydrangea. Upstairs is an L-shaped sofa upholstered in all-weather fabric with a mix of patterned throw pillows. Cosmopolitan and chic, the house has a distinct personality that now reflects the client's voice—always my ultimate decorating goal.

OPPOSITE: In the dining room, an antique Swedish painted rococo chair and a 1940s gilt metal sconce are set against seafoam green walls in a combed plaster. PREVIOUS PAGE: An early-nineteenth-century Italian Piedmontese chandelier hangs above an eighteenth-century Louis XVI dining table. Custom reproduction chairs were inspired by the antique Swedish armchair (opposite). The sleek bone-inlaid Parsons table and cutouts by the celebrated artist Kara Walker create a delicate balance between history and modernity. FOLLOWING PAGES: A provocative photograph of a giant caterpillar by Brazilian artist Fernando Laszlo adds an avant-garde element to the otherwise serene living room, with its mix of custom furniture and eighteenth-century European antiques.

ABOVE: The first-floor landing evokes the home's eclectic spirit with a French 1940s chandelier, Moroccan sconces, nineteenth-century Chinese marble stools, and a custom bench upholstered in bright blue cotton velvet. Candida Höfer's photograph is a room within a room that expands the windowless space.

OPPOSITE: A Queen Anne gilt gesso mirror hangs over one of the five antique mantels purchased for the house. Two 1920s sconces illuminate the Venetian plaster walls that fluctuate between blue, lavender, or gray, depending on the time of day. I am attracted to chameleon colors that change with the light.

PREVIOUS PAGES: The Northern Italian antique chandelier with Murano glass beads in the living room is in harmony with its sister chandelier in the dining room. The custom brown and cream wool rug, which I designed based on an eighteenth-century Portuguese carpet, is a foil for an armless sofa in ivory linen and a 1940s French gilt metal coffee table by Ramsay. FOLLOWING PAGES: The entry foyer has a large 1950s black and polished steel French mirror above a Jansen sofa upholstered in graphic brown and ivory ikat by Dedar. A contemporary painting by Yayoi Kusama is paired with a Russian eighteenth-century commode.

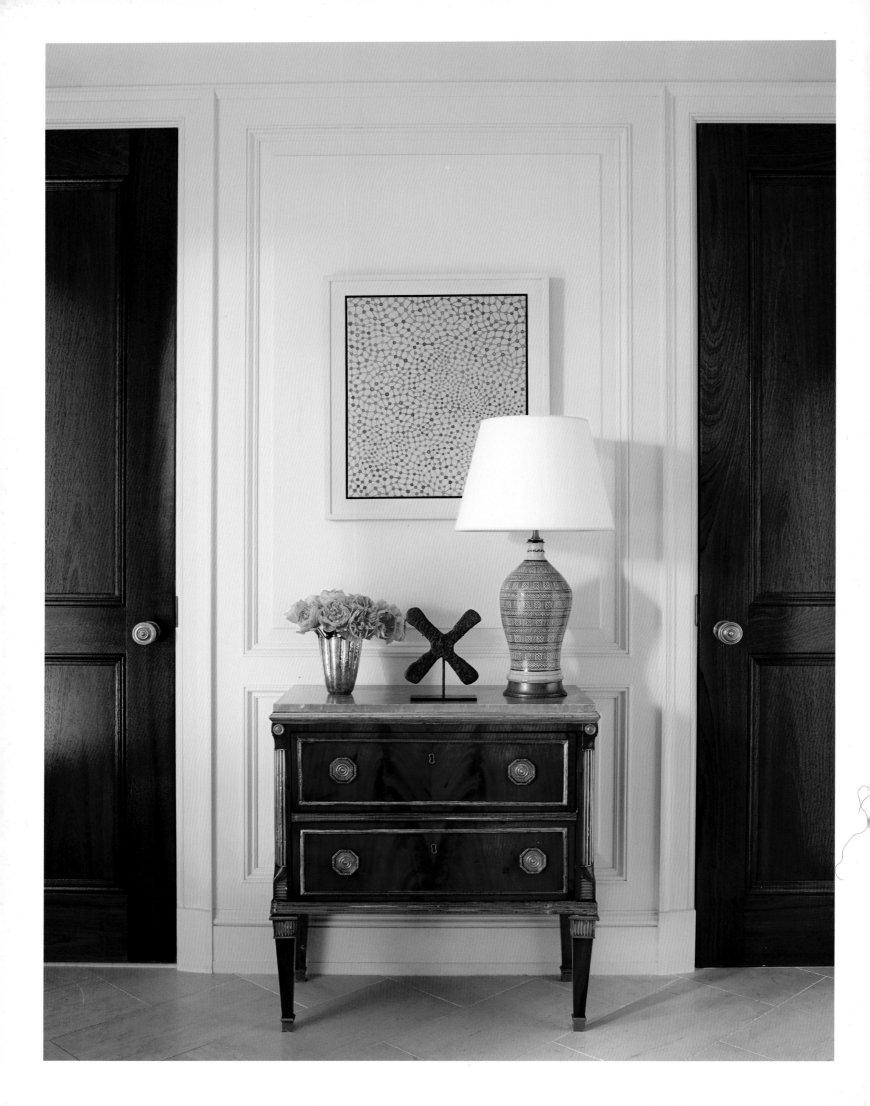

Decorating is
a balancing
act—antique
and modern,
polished and
chalky. Those
are the kinds of
juxtapositions
that make design
interesting.

The eat-in kitchen has a large photograph by German artist
Elger Esser over a custom dining table. The chairs are
mahogany and rattan with chartreuse faux-leather seats.
The light fixture is Italian from the 1950s by Gino Sarfatti.
FOLLOWING PAGES: In the master bedroom, a custom-
colored gray and white David Hicks fabric was quilted
for the bed and armchairs; it was also used for the
curtains. A Gustavian bench is paired with a flokati rug.
The landscape photograph is by Elger Esser.

A jaunty brown and cream striped awning creates an upbeat
mood on the top-floor terrace with a sectional sofa in all-weather
fabric from Kravet. The poufs are vintage Moroccan. A boxwood
hedge creates a green border. PREVIOUS PAGES: In the daughter's
bedroom, the custom four-poster bed has a whimsical canopy
in Osborne & Little linen and a grasscloth headboard, which gives
the bed a contrasting texture. The soft pink wallpaper is by the
British designer Neisha Crosland. A contemporary Venetian
chandelier hangs overhead. The lower-level patio off the daughter's
bedroom has a lighthearted spirit with vintage Sculptura
wire chairs and a teak lattice fence with climbing hydrangea.

46

HAMPTONS GLASS HOUSE

This modernist glass house in the

estate section of Southampton was showing its age when my clients bought it, but the basic design was right on: the interior had wide, open spaces with window walls framing views of a broad lawn and majestic trees. I planned a facelift that would incorporate some vintage furniture and preserve the integrity of the architecture while making it contemporary, easygoing, and family friendly.

The house has two adjoining living areas divided by a two-sided stone fireplace and a shallow set of steps. I designed the spaces to be distinct yet stylistically in sync. Both have a Zen-like quality, but the lower living area has pops of color, with a baby grand piano (one child is a musical prodigy), a pair of 1970s armchairs in a graphic Swedish fabric, and a swivel chair all by Milo Baughman. The upper living room feels relaxed, with a B&B Italia sectional slipcovered in a nubby white fabric. I painted the original white window frames gunmetal gray to outline the views and then used gradations of gray for the walls.

In all my projects, art is indispensable to finishing the rooms. With abundant sunlight, there was only one spot where I could hang a photograph. I chose an abstracted chromogenic print in green and white by the German artist Frank Thiel; poetic and visually powerful, it relates to the views while not being too obviously referential. In the master bedroom, a black and white painting by Sam Messenger adds a layer of intricate texture and visual depth over the custom webbed headboard. Even in the boys' room, the art is part of the design—a psychedelic Victor Vasarely print and decorative prints with a sea motif complete the room.

Arguably, the most striking improvements are the new infinity pool and broad terrace that can be seen from nearly every room. My design of the interiors takes advantage of the unobstructed vistas of greenery, the mature family of evergreen Cryptomeria that surround the house, and the sky beyond.

OPPOSITE: The entry has a beachy Scandinavian modern feel with a pair of pony-skin ottomans beneath a cerused oak table on a natural abaca rug with a linen binding. The large mirror with a bronze frame reflects the abundant natural light. PREVIOUS PAGE: In the dining room, which opens to the kitchen and upper living room, I designed a white lacquer table with oak banding to complement the vintage Robsjohn-Gibbings chairs upholstered with durable apple-green faux leather. The B&B Italia light fixture evokes a constellation at night. The hand-blocked sheer linen curtains are especially beautiful when the light filters through them. FOLLOWING PAGES: In the upper level of the living room, a B&B Italia sectional with form-fitting slipcovers can be reconfigured if the owners choose. The space is kept simple with vintage Poul Kjaerholm chairs and a dark walnut coffee table inspired by Charlotte Perriand.

A vintage Milo Baughman swivel chair is a fun period piece beside the painting by Markus Linnenbrink. OPPOSITE: A photograph by Frank Thiel, from Sean Kelly Gallery, has a three-dimensional quality and is visible from the foyer. FOLLOWING PAGES: The windows have discreet solar shades but were left bare to drink in the view. The vintage 1970s armchairs are upholstered in a graphic Country Swedish green and white fabric. The sofa with roping on the side is based on a modernist Brazilian design. The throw pillows are in a Josef Hoffmann fabric.

Ethereal ivories, creams, pale grays, and blues mixed with a glint of Lucite create a sense of tranquility that is perfect for a bedroom.

Multiple textures are used in the monochromatic master suite with a soft cream bouclé carpet. A painting by Sam Messenger from Maxwell Davidson Gallery hangs over the bed with a webbed headboard and a long pillow in a fabric designed by Analisse Taft. The pony-hair bench has Lucite legs, and the two-tone brass vintage Karl Springer lamps have a wonderful patina.

A guest room, with wall-to-wall sisal carpet in a zigzag pattern, doubles as an office. The desk with iron and wood legs is by McGuire, and the Billy Haines upholstered armchairs are vintage.

The powder room has graphic gray and white wallpaper, which we used as a backdrop to hang shadow boxes with nautical motifs. OPPOSITE: In the sons' room, the beds are upholstered in red linen with white cotton piping, with a Victor Vasarely print on the nesting tables between them. The fabric on the benches and pillows is by Martyn Lawrence Bullard. FOLLOWING PAGES: The house is oriented toward the backyard, where Edmund Hollander reconfigured the terraces and designed a new infinity pool.

MONACO VILLA

Monaco is a principality of high-rises

on the Côte d'Azur, and my longtime clients' private villa is a glamorous anomaly. They were moving here from their London town house (see page 138), and we wanted to integrate some of the art, antiques, and furniture from their previous home. Our goal was a high/low mix that is simple, comfortable, and elegant.

The four-story, early-twentieth-century house, romantically known as Villa Nocturne, required a gut renovation. Collaborating with two architects and the Italian landscape designer Guido Toschi Marazzani Visconti, we expanded and reoriented the house, moving the entry and making the new conservatory and garden the focal points.

While the term *curated* is often misused these days, it's an apt description for the multicultural living room. We reupholstered my clients' Jansen chairs in a chocolate brown and white David Hicks fabric, giving them a more spirited character. We mixed custom kilim rugs, an antique Chinese altar table, slipcovered sofas, a Roman torso, and a contemporary photograph of an old concert hall in Gary, Indiana, which looks like a classical ruin. The natural linen flax curtains are embellished with custom embroidery—the kind of detail that elevates an otherwise simple curtain treatment and adds a layer of richness.

The dining room is similarly curated, with a balanced mix of old and new. A modern table designed by Brazilian architect Arthur Casas is surrounded by chairs slipcovered in a vibrant Dedar fabric. The owners wanted to keep their rather grand giltwood side tables, so I paired them with industrial mirrors. The deceptively simple bronze chandeliers, made in Paris, are lined in gold, casting a magical glow on the ceiling. To warm up the rather Spartan kitchen, I covered the walls in a geometric-patterned black and cream grasscloth and hung powerful photographs of tribal warriors that also line the passage to the dining room.

I always start a project by looking out the windows, which more often than not informs my design decisions for the interiors. The master bedroom's palette was influenced by the view of the French mountainside beyond the garden and the Mediterranean to the south. We painted the walls a stone color called Cornforth White by Farrow & Ball. The room is spare but cozy, with indigo high-pile wall-to-wall carpet and a headboard and curtains made from the same raw silk fabric. The triumph of the renovation is the flow between the indoor and outdoor space, and the way the interior connects with the garden: an enchanting private living room in an urban setting.

OPPOSITE: A new conservatory designed in conjunction with architect Luca Bortolotto added space and glamour to the early-twentieth-century house. PREVIOUS PAGE: One of the few freestanding houses remaining in Monaco, Villa Nocturne is especially beguiling at twilight. FOLLOWING PAGES: The conservatory has a breathtaking view of the newly terraced and landscaped garden by Guido Toschi Marazzani Visconti. I custom made the games table and aubergine-leather-covered stitched chairs after a design by Jean-Michel Frank.

The living room is casual, with
linen-upholstered sofas, a custom-
designed Corian cocktail table, and
antique Biedermeier-style étagères.
The plaques of emperors were
bought from the collection of
Delbée Jansen at Christie's Monaco.

Bespoke details, like custom-embroidered trim on the natural flax-linen curtains and the piping on the Jansen armchairs, give the room a tailored sensibility. My custom-designed pouf is covered in suede. A photograph by Andrew Moore is hung on walls painted in Farrow & Ball Hardwick White. Han terra-cotta incense burners are used as jardinières on the eighteenth-century Chinese altar table.

The dining room has a precisely edited eclecticism. Chandeliers by bronzier Philippe Anthonioz hang over a custom table of reclaimed Brazilian wood surrounded by chairs slipcovered in a bold geometric fabric from Dedar. An industrial frame mirror from Homenature hangs next to a nineteenth-century French painting of hounds over the fireplace. OPPOSITE: The table is set with butterfly plates by Damien Hirst from Gagosian Gallery and Hermès flatware.

The well-used library, with oak
shelves inspired by Jean-Michel Frank,
has a bust of architect Charles Garnier
on a nineteenth-century parquet-top
pedestal table. The walnut hall
chairs are mid-twentieth-century
Italian, and the runner is a custom
kilim by Beauvais Carpets.

ABOVE: In the master suite, the headboard is upholstered in the same raw blue silk as the curtains, which have a printed linen border in a Galbraith & Paul fabric. The custom chest is sheathed in biscuit leather. The bed is made with C&C Milano linens and an African textile. OPPOSITE: In the powder room, a Phillip Jeffries grasscloth wallpaper makes the small space compelling.

Moroccan-inspired grasscloth wallpaper by Phillip Jeffries adds warmth to a Spartan kitchen with limestone floors. Vintage chairs are paired with a classic Saarinen table by Knoll. The tribal photographs by Marie-Laure de Decker are hung in the kitchen as well as the hall leading to the dining room. FOLLOWING PAGES: One of the greatest luxuries in Monaco is a large private garden. I mixed Restoration Hardware wicker sofas with custom-made metal tables with marble tops.

LONG ISLAND
COUNTRY
HOUSE

A small, shingled cottage that was once

part of a grand summer estate designed by Grosvenor Atterbury was the starting point for this project. The new house—classic and romantic, with diamond mullions, eyebrow windows, and wisteria climbing up the shingled exterior—takes its vernacular from the original cottage. The interior bows to tradition, with transoms and paneled walls that are a modern take on the early-twentieth-century resort architecture of McKim, Mead & White.

The house is flooded with light, and I played off that by using sun-washed colors in the living room: a soft lime green for the walls, pastel pink linens for the custom sofa, pale lavender lamps, and a sepia-toned printed fabric for the club chairs. The scheme for the dining room was especially crucial because it is visible from the foyer. I wanted it to be laid back because this is, after all, a beach house, but it had to be elegant enough for formal entertaining, too. To give the room a youthful energy, I designed a sleek, white lacquered trestle table surrounded by painted antique Swedish chairs and hung a 1960s white Murano glass chandelier in the center of the room. The result is a dialogue between the pristine and the patinated, as well as a balance between old and new. I designed box-pleated linen slipcovers for the chairs, giving the room an old Southampton feel. A bold black and white photograph provides a graphic element that finishes the room.

One of the ways I made sure that the rooms have a sense of flow was to use hand-blocked fabrics whenever possible—from Carolina Irving's patterned linen for the curtains in the conservatory to Robert Kime's floral linens for the curtains in the master bedroom. We added Madeline Weinrib's geometric cotton to the library, which has oak paneling painted in a beachy, driftwood-hued tan. Although there are many custom details throughout the house, I was careful not to make it feel too "done." I strive to create interiors that evolve and get better with the patina of time.

OPPOSITE: In the foyer, a custom Christian Astuguevieille rope lantern fabricated in Paris hangs over a round abaca rug. A wing chair paired with a cream lacquer table and vintage ceramic lamp sets a welcoming mood. PREVIOUS PAGES: Antique Swedish chairs have custom pleated linen slipcovers, and the custom wing chair is upholstered in linen. The curtains are an Indian printed cotton in French gray and cream. OPENING PAGE: In the dining room, *Lighting Fields*, a photograph by Hiroshi Sugimoto hung on a paneled wall, is a strikingly modern note in a traditional context, and so is the custom lacquered trestle table and the 1960s Vistosi disc chandelier.

An antique settee upholstered in a custom colored Quadrille fabric paired with patinated antique brass floor lamps offers an intimate spot in the enormous foyer. The painted wooden stools made in Cameroon are from Tucker Robbins in New York. The mahogany mirror is from Vicente Wolf. The sconces are by Soane Britain. OPPOSITE: In the living room, an antique Victorian Colonial daybed upholstered in Carolina Irving fabric sits on a "Patchwork" dhurrie rug by Beauvais. The custom vintage-suzani and linen ottoman was a collaboration with Howe in London. The "Mushroom des Mers" mirror by Thomas Boog is from Maison Gerard.

I don't personally believe in having things totally "decorated," as if everything has been done at once. I love layering things from different periods and cultures, mixing the pristine and the patinated.

In the living room, a multipanel watercolor and pencil work on paper by David Thorpe from the Casey Kaplan Gallery hangs on soft lime green walls above a custom sofa in light pink linen. The vintage bleached-wood coffee table is from Amy Perlin Antiques. Custom armchairs are upholstered in a printed fabric by Carolina Irving.

In the conservatory, a custom slipper chair upholstered in a linen stripe from C&C Milano is paired with a gilt standing lamp and vintage suzani pillows. OPPOSITE: A view to the conservatory from the living room. The contemporary color photograph is by Olivo Barbieri from the Yancey Richardson Gallery. The custom marble jardinières were a collaboration with Odegard, Inc. FOLLOWING SPREAD: The curtains are made from an exotic floral linen from Carolina Irving. The Parsons-style poured concrete coffee table is finished in a modeled gray paint. The vintage card table is Swedish from the 1940s.

In the master bedroom, a vintage Danish armchair is upholstered in a soft blue wool bouclé. The pinch-pleat curtains are in a Robert Kime fabric. OPPOSITE: A photograph by Darren Almond from Love Fine Art Inc. hangs above the white lacquer four-poster bed that I designed. FOLLOWING PAGES: Inspired by the cottage's original window design by Grosvenor Atterbury, a crisscross window sits above the reading nook. In the master bathroom, utilitarian plumbing fixtures and marble basins are in keeping with the house's history.

Vintage holophane pendants from Remains Lighting hang above the two paneled islands. OPPOSITE: The custom Corian table on a metal base is surrounded by a set of vintage Kaare Klint chairs with their original leather. The Italian wood and metal chandelier adds a touch of whimsy. PRECEDING PAGES: Much of the furniture in the son's room is from catalogs; the bed is by Ballard Designs. The contemporary art adds a sophisticated edge. FOLLOWING PAGES: On the screened-in porch, which looks out to the pool house and pergola, furniture from Munder-Skiles has graphic cushions in an indoor/outdoor fabric by Schumacher. The floor and terraces are made of bluestone, and the paths are in a brick herringbone pattern. The table has Hermès plates and vases from West Elm.

GREENWICH VILLAGE
CLASSIC

The first New York apartment I owned,

in a 1920s limestone and red brick building on lower Fifth Avenue, was on a high floor, with ten-foot ceilings that overlooked the rooftops and steeples of Greenwich Village and the Hudson River beyond. The apartment had an interesting pedigree, having been owned by the MTV veejay Downtown Julie Brown. I was traveling a lot to Europe at the time and was under the spell of Paris, which influenced its design. I wanted to create a peaceful space to come home to. I painted the living room a chameleon lavender-gray, making the blue-gray sky outside feel at one with the interior, and relied on neutrals—creams, straw colors, and cocoa chocolate brown—for the furnishings.

I wanted the rooms to feel layered yet airy, so I relied on texture to provide dimension. The foundation for the living room is a sisal rug, hand painted by a Belgian artist with a geometric pattern that plays off the design of the floors in the foyer. I copied the lines of a classic Jansen sofa, updating its look by making the base out of quarter-sawn cerused oak, covering it in a nubby fabric that has the feel of a refined burlap, and trimming it with silver nail heads. The custom white lacquer étagères flanking the fireplace and the glass Hermès coffee table with leather-wrapped legs contribute to the sense of openness. I wanted to use the space in front of the window for both working and dining, so I chose multipurpose furniture: an eighteenth-century English drop-leaf table and metamorphic French campaign chairs from the Paris flea market. I then had four copies made that could be folded up and brought out for dinner parties. The intimate kitchen had enough space for a seating nook upholstered in a Manuel Canovas toile. All the wood floors were bleached and stained for a light Scandinavian feel, but in the kitchen we uncovered, during the renovation, the original cement floors, which I then had refurbished; this little surprise was exactly right for the room.

The bedroom is painted a warm limestone color, and the carpet is a classic 1960s design that I custom colored. The western light filters through the unlined, oversize, checked linen curtains. The white cotton bed is dressed with cashmere pillows and throws. The Adnet leather-covered lamp stands like a piece of sculpture over the armchair upholstered in thick natural linen. Above the bed, an Ellsworth Kelly lithograph—a spare line drawing of a flower—captures the essence of the apartment's simple sensibility.

OPPOSITE: The apartment's prewar character was enhanced with the addition of panel moldings, and the neutral palette expands the space. A vintage mirror from Mecox Gardens hangs over the fireplace flanked by two modern custom wing chairs and custom white lacquer étagères. The glass and leather coffee table is by Jacques Adnet for Hermès. PREVIOUS PAGE: A 1940s crystal and mirror console sparkles in the entry hall, which has wood floors stenciled in a geometric pattern I designed and had painted in collaboration with the artist Monique Denoncin.

Proportion, along with color and texture, is key to the living room's sense of calm and order. The fauteuil is upholstered in a glazed linen. The patinated plaster 1930s shell sconce is by Jean-Charles Moreux, and lithographs over the sofa are by Agnes Martin. OPPOSITE: An eighteenth-century English drop-leaf table and French campaign chairs are unfolded for dining. PREVIOUS PAGES: The furniture is arranged on a custom-painted sisal carpet. The sofa is a reinterpretation of a Jansen design trimmed with oak and silver nail heads.

The kitchen's original cement floor was uncovered and refurbished. The new
glass-fronted cabinets are a nod to history. OPPOSITE: An English tripod table is
used for breakfast at the banquette upholstered in a Manuel Canovas toile.

The bedroom is an essay in tone-on-tone decorating in creams and browns. An Ellsworth Kelly print hangs above the linen-upholstered bed. The wool carpet is inspired by a David Hicks design, and the curtains are a Rogers & Goffigon cookies-and-cream checked linen. The chair and ottoman are upholstered in Belgian linen, and the leather-clad reading lamp is by Jacques Adnet.

UPPER EAST SIDE
DUPLEX

It may seem counterintuitive, but when

confronted with a room that has extraordinarily high ceilings, I focus on the floor first: it's important to bring your eye down. The narrow living room of this duplex apartment has a twenty-six-foot-high ceiling. My first step was to add a Renaissance-inspired stenciled floor in shades of brown that required painstaking work by a decorative painter. I then added a patterned rug to layer in a contemporary attitude. Since the room faces north, I decided to forgo curtains, because too much fabric would detract from the inherent drama of the sky-high, original iron windows. This vertical space presented a great opportunity for a piece of art. A mobile with the poetic title, *A Library of Leaves*, that has etched into it the words "One Moment Sheds Light on the Other" was the perfect denouement for this room.

The regular-height dining room and library flank the living room, and each has its own personality. I thought of the dining room as an extension of the kitchen, so it had to be suitable for everyday use as well as special occasions. I custom colored a hand-painted de Gournay wallpaper, and designed a faux-shagreen table surrounded by klismos chairs in plum pleather, which can be wiped down in case of a spill. The library has a rich, cozy feeling, wrapped with aubergine lacquered bookshelves whose backs are painted in the same contrasting color as the ceiling. An abstract Japanese mixed-paper collage by Kenzo Okada over the sofa beckons you into the room and lightens the ambience. Instead of matching sofas, I added a daybed that can accommodate an overnight guest and makes the seating arrangement more interesting.

My approach to master bedrooms is fairly consistent: they must be soothing and peaceful, but they can have a quiet glamour, too. Here, I chose a hand-painted wallpaper that reminds me of a Gerhard Richter painting. I hung it on the horizontal to expand the feeling of the room. The headboard is a hybrid—inspired by Venetian and English versions—and so is the settee that combines Swedish and French 1940s style. I like nothing more than taking cues from the classics and giving them a modern twist. The home is a beautiful paradox: fresh and familiar, low-key and luxurious, traditional and original.

OPPOSITE: In the twenty-six-foot-high living room, the north-facing casement window was left bare to showcase its dramatic size and patina. The hand-painted floors in a Renaissance pattern add visual depth and interest to this towering space. The custom chairs that flank the fireplace are as high as the mantel, while the Napolean-style sofa upholstered in a dark gray silk velvet is low-slung, which makes the room more dynamic. PREVIOUS PAGE: A mobile by Martin Boyce gracefully and provocatively takes advantage of the space without dominating it. The photograph of Trinity Library by Candida Höfer over the sofa is a nod to the room's sky-high window.

The dining room, with classic
hand-painted Chinese de Gournay
wallpaper, is used for everyday family
meals as well as special occasions.
I designed a faux-shagreen table and
oak klismos chairs with faux-leather
seats. Above this, I hung a clear English
glass chandelier from the 1920s.
A pair of round brass mirrors hangs
over the antique Swedish chests.
FOLLOWING PAGES: The library has
aubergine lacquered paneled walls
and bookshelves with backs painted
the same stone color as the ceiling.

The windowed dressing niche has a Corian dressing table, a polished nickel light fixture from Galerie des Lampes, a plaster mirror, and a custom chair covered in a Romo fabric. OPPOSITE: Wallpaper that is reminiscent of a Gerhard Richter painting gives the master bedroom an ethereal ambience. The linen-velvet headboard trimmed in nail heads is a hybrid of English and Venetian styles. The gilt metal and travertine table and settee inspired by French and Swedish design are set in front of the television. PREVIOUS PAGES: I designed a tall, high-gloss lacquered Parsons table in the kitchen, which serves for both meal preparation and casual dining. The daughter's bedroom has a retro 1970s feel, with graphic wallpaper and buoyant floral fabric for the shades and benches.

LONDON
TOWN HOUSE

I love working in London, where the

architecture and history never fail to spark the imagination. In collaboration with architect Jamie Fobert, we restored many of the original features of this early-nineteenth-century house on Montagu Square, while adding some modern architectural details. One of its best attributes was the cantilevered Portland stone staircase that was in disrepair, and we found the original quarry to restore the treads. The house had all its original solid mahogany doors that I had restored with a period wax finish.

We respected tradition and referenced history while reimagining this home for the twenty-first century. We made several forays to the Sir John Soane's Museum in search of inspiration. Since the house is Grade II listed and protected by English Heritage, we couldn't replace the chimneypieces, but we could swap them, so the mantel from the dining room is now in the drawing room and vice versa. I contrasted the grander elements in the living room— an eighteenth-century George III gilt-carton Pierre Mirror, Louis XVI ormolu sconces, eighteenth-century plaster busts—with painted ivory walls, a neutral carpet with a Greek key pattern, twentieth-century armchairs, and unadorned raw-silk curtains.

The dining room was designed around the important Fonthill Splendens chimneypiece. The tangerine Irish wool and linen upholstered walls provide a textured backdrop for the monumental mantel that functions as a piece of sculpture in this formal space. I paired an early-nineteenth-century mahogany twin-pedestal table with Regency chairs and a set of four 1950s giltwood wall lights. The restrained cut-glass chandelier is a copy of an early-eighteenth-century English model. It's a classic room that, despite all the antiques, feels light and fresh. The clean-lined master bedroom with grayish-tan walls was influenced by the art deco period; I designed a limestone stepped chimneypiece, Ruhlmann-inspired sconces, and a geometric corner screen to balance the room's proportions. A 1940s French mirror, a glass Jacques Adnet table, and vintage Lucite obelisks all have a modern attitude.

When my clients moved to a smaller house in Monaco (page 68), we sold much of their furniture and decorative objects at a Christie's auction that also featured the collections of two of my favorite designers: Jansen and David Hicks. My section of the sale was dubbed "The Property of a Gentleman," which was appropriate for this client, who cherishes his privacy. Our pursuit of beauty continued with the decoration of their Monaco home.

OPPOSITE: In the drawing room, a pair of Maison Jansen chairs upholstered in a striated cotton velvet is placed in front of a George III chimneypiece that was formerly in the dining room. Floor-to-ceiling donkey-gray raw-silk curtains are paired with ivory walls. PREVIOUS PAGE: The treads on the cantilevered staircase were restored with Portland stone from the same quarry where the originals were found. Louis XVI engravings of the military battles of Emperor Qianlong are hung on the stairwell walls painted in Farrow & Ball Elephant's Breath. The George II gilt console is eighteenth century and the George III mirror is by John Vardy. FOLLOWING PAGES: In the landing outside the master bedroom, a nineteenth-century collector's cabinet contains an exquisite assortment of shells. A terra-cotta bust of Charles Garnier, who designed the Monaco and Paris opera houses, is set in front of a North Italian chinoiserie parcel-gilt and painted mirror. Two custom armchairs are placed on either side of a Regency center table. The artwork is a Chinese eighteenth-century drawing of a melancholy horse from the Chinese Porcelain Company.

As a kid, I spent every cent I earned from my paper route at auction houses. The first thing I ever bought was a George II mahogany chair with a needlepoint seat— I was twelve.

The guest room has camel's hair walls and a French Directoire campaign bed with a canopy in red and white ticking. The bedcover is an antique Persian textile. PREVIOUS PAGES: The library's bookshelves, inspired by those at Sir John Soane's Museum in London, were designed in conjunction with architect Jamie Fobert. The impressive Fonthill Splendens chimneypiece serves as a sculptural focal point to the dining room. I restored the original mahogany doors and hardware and upholstered the walls in a tangerine linen and wool fabric woven in Ireland.

The tub is set into thick limestone with a matching stone counter. The photograph is by German photographer Dietmar Busse. OPPOSITE: The 1930s mirror in the master bedroom adds sparkle to the monochromatic room, with grayish tan walls and a chaise upholstered in wool. The mirrored table is Jacques Adnet. I designed the custom cream-painted wood screen, which camouflages the asymmetry of the chimneypiece sidewalls.

I like interiors that have a bit of patina but are still very crisp.

The garden room has a modern attitude that is refreshing for a historic house. The brass-studded vintage velvet mirror is French, and the brass and blue-glass wall lights by Marc du Plantier are circa 1940. The coffee table is eighteenth-century Chinese. A suite of prints by Sean Scully hangs above the custom sofa.

PARK AVENUE
PREWAR

Avenue are inherently dignified, but in the twenty-first century they must have a modern attitude. My fashionable client and her husband were moving from a downtown loft to a "Classic 8," and they wanted their new residence to be elegant and effervescent. Since the apartment (once owned by the pioneering broadcaster Barbara Walters) required a gut renovation, I worked with architect Leonard Woods to tweak the original layout, while maintaining the classic architecture and enfilade of public rooms.

The windowless front hall was reconfigured to be airy, gracious, and whimsical. Inspired by eighteenth-century Swedish wallpaper I'd seen in Drottningholm Palace, I commissioned a decorative artist to paint fanciful trees on a textured, chalky cream and white background (my vision was Jack in the Beanstalk in eighteenth-century Scandinavia). I grounded the space with a Madeline Weinrib trellis-patterned rug and then layered in an antique Swedish table, a Colonial Brazilian bench, grass-green David Hicks stools, and Gothic-inspired lanterns fabricated in London. The living room is similarly idiosyncratic. Armchairs upholstered in a Persian floral textile flank a coffee table fashioned from an antique Chinese daybed. An elaborate art deco mirror hangs above the simple Louis XVI chimneypiece. Luxurious textured ivory curtains with hand-embroidered bespoke trim are contrasted with a humble abaca rug. And a corner banquette covered in cocoa-brown Ultrasuede has a downtown vibe for casual entertaining.

The home's unique personality is evident in the dining room, with its combination of a Persian rug, an Irish mahogany table, a blown-glass chandelier, and an abstract artwork by Hurvin Anderson. The book-filled library, paneled with reclaimed pine, has a contemporary edge thanks to the large-scale, black and white work on paper by Richard Serra. In the refined master bedroom, the curtains are made of bold Lulu DK fabric that was also used to cover the custom bench at the foot of the leather-upholstered bed. The apartment's eclecticism offers the owners a great place to raise their children and to entertain in a fashion that suits their unique sense of style.

OPPOSITE: The apartment's artful mix is evident in this living room vignette, with a carved and painted Swedish Gustavian demilune table, a patinated swing-arm lamp, an abstract stone sculpture, and a work on paper by Sigmar Polke. PREVIOUS PAGES: The expansive foyer is a welcoming room, with walls painted in a whimsical Jack-in-the-Beanstalk design inspired by eighteenth-century Swedish wallpaper. The medley of furnishings includes original Billy Baldwin slipper chairs upholstered in a Les Indiennes printed cotton, a Colonial Brazilian bench, a Swedish table, an English lantern, and a trellis rug by Madeline Weinrib. OPENING PAGE: Gilt metal sconces flank a twentieth-century Venetian mirror over the Louis XVI limestone mantelpiece.

I try to give my clients something classic yet unpretentious, that meshes the worlds of uptown and downtown, high and low.

In the dining room, a painting by Hurvin Anderson is a contemporary counterpoint to the Persian rug, Irish mahogany table, and custom chairs with backs upholstered in red grasscloth. PREVIOUS PAGES: Painted a soft, waxed Venetian plaster finish, the living room is a spirited mélange with Bridgewater chairs upholstered in a Lee Jofa ivory and blue Persian-inspired fabric, a custom corner banquette and sofa, and cream-colored curtains with embroidered bespoke trim.

The powder room is covered in geometric faux-wood wallpaper by Maya Romanoff. The Venetian-style mirror and gilt metal sconces create an intimate mood. OPPOSITE: In the library, a work on paper by Richard Serra is hung on walls with reclaimed pine paneling. The sofa, covered in striped velvet by Old World Weavers, is accompanied by an oversize cowhide ottoman. FOLLOWING PAGES: The wife's dressing table has a skirt in gray and white printed cotton fabric and a vintage Lucite bench. The elegant master suite, painted a soft blue, has a leather bed trimmed in nail heads and a 1940s Italian chandelier with rock crystal and amethyst stones. An exuberant Lulu DK print was used for the curtains and bench.

SUTTON PLACE TOWN HOUSE

I am always inspired and challenged by

clients with vision and inquisitive minds. The late media mogul William Reilly loved history, and designing his Sutton Square town house was a privilege because he set out to create "one of the great houses in New York City." The project began in 1991 with an imposing Georgian town house on the East River; three years later, we combined it with an adjacent residence that allowed Bill to live and entertain in grand style. His parties were remarkable. He expected his guests to be great conversationalists. He liked nothing more than dinner parties with informed and witty repartee.

We imported double-hung sash windows from Ireland, covered the public room floors in antique oak parquet de Versailles, and commissioned custom hardware from P.E. Guerin. We went on buying trips together, traveling to Ireland, Sweden, and London for the annual Grosvenor House Art & Antiques Fair. We painted the living room walls a deep Farrow & Ball brown and the baseboards a battleship gray, so all the eighteenth- and nineteenth-century gilt furniture would shine. I designed custom upholstery at the right scale for such a large room. In the summers, just like they do in great European manor houses, we switched out the Oriental rugs for sisal and slipcovered the chairs and sofas in gray and white ticking, giving the room an entirely different, fresh look.

The dining room was baronial but warm and welcoming, too. In England I found a beautifully patinated, unusually large Irish mahogany hunt table that we surrounded with six George II walnut side chairs (and six exact reproductions commissioned from an English furniture maker). In summer, they're dressed in coral and white gingham slipcovers. There were two other elements that made the room especially breathtaking: an early nineteenth-century Italian chimneypiece and a jubilant sixteenth-century painting of the commedia dell'arte. It's impossible to discuss this house without mentioning the staircase that spirals broadly through the center, which is lit by an enormous lantern suspended from an immense multi-paned, domed skylight. After Bill passed away in 2008, the contents of this very personal home were auctioned off at a single-owner Christie's sale in 2009, but the memory of this grand house is indelible.

OPPOSITE: In the living room, a custom curved sofa with gray and white striped summer slipcovers is set into the window bay that overlooks the East River. The side chairs are eighteenth-century Russian, and the coffee table is French, circa 1970s. PREVIOUS PAGE: A marble sculpture of Aphrodite from the Hellenistic period is at the center of the foyer that is illuminated during the day by a massive skylight. The chairs are eighteenth-century Louis XVI giltwood fauteuils. FOLLOWING PAGES: The living room has a George III neoclassical chimneypiece. The sofas are dressed in their summer slipcovers. A cut-glass and hexagonal lantern from northern Europe hangs over the Regency Pollard oak library table.

The dining room is lit by a nineteenth-century Italian giltwood chandelier. The eighteenth-century George II walnut dining room chairs are dressed in summer slipcovers in a coral and cream large-scale cotton gingham. OPPOSITE: An ancient Roman marble portrait head of the young Marcus Aurelius is set on the library table in the living room surrounded by early-eighteenth-century English walnut stools.

Dining room chairs, upholstered in a gauffraged custom-colored silk velvet by Claremont, surround the late-eighteenth-century Irish George III mahogany hunt table. The mantelpiece is early-nineteenth-century Italian.

In the library, the walls are decorative-painted in
an old-fashioned milk paint. The furniture
includes early-nineteenth-century mahogany and
caned bergères and a late-eighteenth-century Louis
XVI ormolu-mounted mahogany bureau plat.

THE OXFORD HISTORY OF CLASSICAL ART

CLASSICAL ART

NEW YORK

Treasures of the Art Museum of Irkutsk

FABERGÉ: IMPERIAL JEWELER
VON HABSBURG AND LOPATO

ERNEST HEMINGWAY REDISCOVERED

GAUGUIN A RETROSPECTIVE

CHINA: THE LONG MARCH

A mix of vintage and custom embroidered pillows adds a dose of color to the library sofa, upholstered in a neutral ottoman fabric. OPPOSITE: Antique Persian textiles are integrated as trim on the wool camel's hair curtains and valance. A white marble bust of Benjamin Franklin is set on a nineteenth-century northern European walnut cupboard.

In the master suite, the custom black-painted and parcel-gilt four-poster bed has turned posts and a rectangular canopy. The work by Sean Scully and the framed Egyptian textiles add a contemporary counterpoint to the fine antiques.

The master bathroom is covered in bookmatched Calacatta marble. The custom lime-washed oak stools inspired by Jean-Michel Frank have terrycloth seat covers. The black and white drawings on the walls are by Ellsworth Kelly.

CONNECTICUT COUNTRY HOUSE

The prerevolutionary towns of Litchfield

County are known for their rural landscape of rolling hills and historic clapboard farmhouses. Working with architect Timothy Bryant, we designed a new house based on an eighteenth-century Colonial. Overlooking a pristine lake at the end of a long, winding driveway flanked by an apple orchard, the house is contextual and well proportioned; my goal was to decorate it with a nod to the past while making it practical for the present.

When decorating newly built houses, I often use pieces with a patina that convey a sense of history. In this instance, I found threadbare Oriental rugs and turned vintage ceramics into lamps. An antique English chest and iron chandelier create a balance between old and new in the entry hall, which we painted my custom warm white to make the architectural details pop against the dark wood floors. I used Farrow & Ball paints throughout because they give a sense of depth and instant character. In the living room, I painted the walls a subtle putty gray-green, juxtaposing skirted sofas upholstered in ocher wool fabric with antiques, such as a painted Swedish clock, an oak cricket table, and an English mahogany sofa table. A clamming basket for firewood is a simple rustic touch. The dining area has a colonial Brazilian table surrounded by Rose Tarlow chairs slipcovered in a mustard and cream check beneath a spare yet fanciful iron chandelier. The oil-rubbed bronze curtain rods and hardware in the kitchen also contribute to the home's equilibrium.

The first-floor master bedroom has a vaulted, paneled ceiling painted a slipper satin white, and everything is in restful shades of ivory, blue, and green. I used the same wool fabric for the headboard, loveseat, and Roman shades, which makes the room cohesive. The reproduction Swedish night tables and nineteenth-century English caned bench contribute to the collected look.

In the side entrance that is used by the family on a daily basis, I contrasted antiques—a faded runner, an English hall bench, and glass and metal lanterns—with the crisp white woodwork. Altogether, the feeling is classic, airy, and up to date.

OPPOSITE: The new clapboard Colonial required a decorating scheme that would complement the traditional exterior. PREVIOUS PAGE: The historic New England vernacular calls for simplicity, so the stairs were left bare to showcase the architectural details. A lamp made from an antique ceramic jug is paired with an English oak chest in the foyer.

The kitchen opens into the family room. Antique English holophanes from Ann-Morris hang from a paneled ceiling. The kitchen is painted my custom white that I developed with Donald Kaufman. PREVIOUS PAGES: In the living room, an antique Sultanabad rug was the starting point. Skirted custom sofas upholstered in rich ocher wool are appropriately relaxed for this country house.

Dark floors contrasted with light fabrics in the family room create a warm, fresh mood. The dining table is colonial Brazilian, and the chairs are from Rose Tarlow. FOLLOWING PAGES: The scheme for the family room has depth and warmth despite the light palette. The sofa is a custom English scroll arm, the table is from John Rosselli, and the linen-and-wool-blend curtains are Schumacher. The well-worn Sultanabad rug adds a layer of patina.

I don't like interiors that look wrong when the client starts adding things. I strive to create comfort-able spaces that evolve—rooms that get better with time.

The master bedroom has a peaked, paneled ceiling with unlined curtains and blackout shades for sleeping. Reproduction nightstands flank the bed with a blue wool headboard. Photographs by Jeffrey Conley hang on the walls, which are painted in Farrow & Ball Clunch.

The master bathroom is clean and crisp, with paneled walls, handsome moldings, and an antique rug. The mirrors are custom designed and painted, the polished nickel sconces are from Ann-Morris, and the alabaster bowl is by Vaughan. OPPOSITE: More than a mudroom, the side entrance is a proper entry, with an antique English bench and lanterns from Vaughan. FOLLOWING PAGES: The master bedroom is a pared-down take on classic New England style. We copied a nineteenth-century English armchair and covered it in vintage linen. Caldwell sconces from the 1920s flank an antique round English mahogany mirror.

SOUTHAMPTON
COTTAGE

My weekend home is a light-filled, 1914

shingled cottage in the village of Southampton, New York. What sold me on the property was the sunny yard with plenty of room for vegetable and cutting gardens. The existing property was in serious need of new landscaping, and I like getting my hands dirty—it has been very satisfying to watch the newly planted hydrangeas become lush and the privet hedge grow thick to provide a natural privacy screen. Above all, the house was manageable, so I could putter in the garden, kick back, and decompress. Spending time there allows me to connect with nature, which always inspires my design work.

When I'm my own client, I have complete freedom of expression. I wanted to have fun with colors here, so I painted the living room a soft pink and my bedroom a Benjamin Moore pale lavender that whispers baby blue. Everything is colorful yet paradoxically subtle and soothing. I didn't rip out the kitchen, as others might have, but I did give it a face-lift by painting the existing bead-board cabinets in a crisp white so the kitchen feels bright and cheerful even on an overcast day. I painted the existing Victorian hall piece in the foyer white, so it now has a stunning, sculptural, Louise Nevelson–like presence against the deep indigo raffia walls. I designed a Lucite table to make the small dining room feel expansive—an unexpected modern touch that enlivens the traditional cottage.

I wanted the house to have a fresh farmhouse spirit, so I mixed in a lot of contemporary art. On the wall along the staircase are three poetic black and white photographs by Francesca Woodman; in the living room, fern prints by Giuseppe Penone framed in Plexiglas cover the pink walls like wallpaper; a color photograph by Jenny van Sommers hangs over the guest room bed.

The house has Moroccan and Turkish influences, reflecting my love of travel. I used hand-woven abaca rugs from the Philippines and vintage kilims from Iran, as well as Spanish lamps with shades made of twine that create wonderful patterns on the walls when they are lit at night. The Portuguese-inspired four-poster bed makes the room feel taller and larger than it actually is. I think a weekend house should be a change of pace in every way, and this cottage offers a welcome contrast from my urbane Manhattan apartment (page 14).

OPPOSITE: In a corner of the living room, painted in Pink Ground by Farrow & Ball, a vintage white lacquer chest is paired with a 1960s caned chair by Harvey Probber, giving the traditional home a modern edge. The fern prints by Giuseppe Penone are a contemporary take on the botanical genre. PREVIOUS PAGE: In a beach house, walking barefoot is the norm, so I used textured rugs on smooth chocolate brown floors for an easygoing ambience.

A striped cotton dhurrie runner from Madeline Weinrib on the staircase has the same indigo hue as the walls covered in raffia from Phillip Jeffries. OPPOSITE: Painted my custom white from Donald Kaufman, the original banister and Victorian hall piece look like sculptural elements against the dark walls. The "Ornamental Sphere" light fixture is a reproduction of a French 1950s design. PREVIOUS PAGES: In the living room, custom Bridgewater sofas are upholstered in a chocolate and ivory woven fabric from C&C Milano. The throw pillows were made from vintage suzanis and chocolate and ivory striped alpaca. The suede ottoman is my custom design.

The dining room feels open and modern, with my custom Lucite dining table by Plexi-Craft and vintage caned chairs by Harvey Probber with custom seat cushions. The circa-1920 wood and iron chandelier is from France. A mixed-media seascape by Silvia Rivas hangs on the pale pink walls above an antique painted Swedish buffet. The antique brass wall lights are from Soane Britain.

I like color that gradually reveals itself, and no color has the capacity to do that quite like complex whites.

The existing bead-board cabinets were painted a crisp Benjamin Moore white, and the trim is Farrow & Ball Cornforth White, which is the perfect feather gray. A contemporary photograph by Go Sugimoto hangs over an English iron and wood table. Sturdy deck paint was used for the checkerboard floor.

Outfitted with fixtures from Waterworks, this newly renovated bathroom has an appropriately vintage feel. The towel warmer is a discreet luxury. OPPOSITE: The master bedroom reflects my wanderlust: the four-poster bed was inspired by a Portuguese bed and made by Martyn Lawrence Bullard; the antique kilim rug is from Iran; the circa-1930 Giacometti-style lamps from Spain have their original wicker shades that create wonderful patterns on the walls, which are painted in Benjamin Moore Polar White.

The teak sofas and chairs beneath the pergola are from
Restoration Hardware, with custom pillows in
all-weather fabric. The two-level reclaimed teak coffee
table is from Mecox Gardens in Southampton, N.Y.

The backyard was landscaped in collaboration with Vickie Cardaro of Buttercup Design Group. A new privet hedge provides privacy. Lava stone planters, an open-sphere sculpture, and a pair of ceramic elephants from Homenature give the outside an inviting, finished look.

RESOURCES

ANTIQUES

1stdibs
1stdibs.com

Alexandre Biaggi
alexandrebiaggi.com

Anne Jaudel, Paris

Anne Sophie Duval
annesophieduval.com

Axel Vervoordt
axel-vervoordt.com

Balsamo Antiques
balsamoantiques.com

Bernd Goeckler
bgoecklerantiques.com

Bermingham & Co.
berminghamantiques.com

BK Antiques
bkantiques.com

Bloom, Sag Harbor

Carlton Hobbs
carltonhobbs.com

Christie's
christies.com

Christopher Howe
howelondon.com

Ciancimino
ciancimino.com

C.J. Peters
cjpeters.net

Cove Landing
1stdibs.com/dealers/cove-landing

David Gill Galleries
davidgillgalleries.com

Demiurge
demiurgenewyork.com

Dienst & Dotter
dienstanddotter.com

Doyle
doylenewyork.com

Duane
duanemodern.com

David Duncan Antiques
davidduncanantiques.com

Eric Appel
ericappel.com

Evergreen Antiques
evergreenantiques.com

Galerie Chastel-Marechal
chastel-marechal.com

Galerie du Passage
galeriedupassage.com

Galerie Dubois, Paris

Galerie Patrick Seguin
patrickseguin.com

Galerie Yves Gastou
galerieyvesgastou.com

Gerald Bland Inc.
geraldblandinc.com

Guinevere
guinevere.co.uk

Hemisphere Antiques
hemisphere-antiques.com

Hostler Burrows
hostlerburrows.com

Jacksons
jacksons.se

J.F. Chen
jfchen.com

John King, London

John Rosselli Antiques
johnrosselliantiques.com

Jonathan Burden
jonathanburden.com

Laserow Antiques
laserowantiques.com

Lief
liefalmont.com

Liz O'Brien
lizobrien.com

Lucca Antiques
luccaantiques.com

Lucca & Co.
luccany.com

LVS Antiquites
lvsantiquites.com

Maison Gerard
maisongerard.com

Mallett Antiques
mallettantiques.com

Niall Smith Antiques
1stdibs.com/dealers/niall-smith-antiques

Patrick Perrin, Paris

Phillips
phillips.com

R. E. Steele
1stdibs.com/dealers/re-steele

Richard L. Feigen & Co.
rlfeigen.com/gallery

Rose Uniacke
roseuniacke.com

Sotheby's
sothebys.com

Venfield
venfieldnyc.com

Vicente Wolf
vicentewolf.com

Wyeth
wyethome.com

ARCHITECTS

Matthew Baird
bairdarchitects.com

Kathleen Baldwin

Luca Bortolotto
lucabortolotto.com

Timothy Bryant
timothybryant.com

Marc Corbiau
corbiau.com

Jamie Fobert
jamiefobertarchitects.com

David Stanton

Leonard Woods
lwarchitect.com

ART

Ameringer McEngery Yohe
amy-nyc.com

Anthony Meier Fine Arts
anthonymeierfinearts.com

Casey Kaplan Gallery
caseykaplangallery.com

Davidson Contemporary
davidsoncontemporary.com

Gagosian Gallery
gagosian.com

Gemini G.E.L.
geminigel.com

Ingleby Gallery
inglebygallery.com

Love Fine Art, Inc.
lovefineartinc.com

Matthew Marks Gallery
matthewmarks.com

Maxwell Davidson Gallery
davidsongallery.com

Marian Goodman Gallery
mariangoodman.com

Mendes Wood DM
mendeswooddm.com

Michael Werner Gallery
michaelwerner.com

Pace Prints
paceprints.com

Sean Kelly Gallery
skny.com

Sonabend Gallery
sonnabendgallery.com

Tanya Bonakdar Gallery
tanyabonakdargallery.com

The Chinese Porcelain Company
chineseporcelaincompany.com

Timothy Taylor Gallery
timothytaylorgallery.com

Yancey Richardson Gallery
yanceyrichardson.com

FABRICS & WALL COVERINGS

ALT for Living
altforliving.com

Antique Textile Collections
antiquetextilescollections.com

Bernard Thorpe
bernardthorp.co.uk

C&C Milano
cec-milano.com

Callidus Guild
callidusguild.com

Carolina Irving
carolinairvingtextiles.com

China Seas
quadrillefabrics.com/chinaseas.html

Christopher Farr
christopherfarr.com

Claremont
claremontfurnishing.com

Clarence House
clarencehouse.com

Cowtan & Tout
cowtan.com

David Hicks
davidhicksfrance.com

Dedar
dedar.com

De Gournay
degournay.com

De Le Cuona
delecuona.co.uk

Donghia
donghia.com

Edelman Leather
edelmanleather.com

Holland & Sherry
interiors.hollandandsherry.com

Idarica Gazzoni
idaricagazzoni.com

John Robshaw
johnrobshaw.com

Galbraith & Paul
galbraithandpaul.com

Knoll
knoll.com

Kravet
kravet.com

Lee Jofa
leejofa.com

Les Indiennes
lesindiennes.com

Loro Piana
loropiana.com

Lulu DK
luludk.com

Mariaflora
mariaflora.com

Martyn Lawrence Bullard for
Schumacher
martynlawrencebullard.com
fschumacher.com

Maya Romanoff
mayaromanoff.com

Marimekko
us.marimekko.com

Merry Mullings
mmdesigntextiles.co

Neisha Crosland
neishacrosland.com

Old World Weavers
starkcarpet.com

Osborne & Little
osborneandlittle.com

Phillip Jeffries
phillipjeffries.com

Quadrille
quadrillefabrics.com

Rogers & Goffigon
rogersandgoffigon.com

Romo
romo.com

S. Harris
sharris.com

Samuel & Sons
samuelandsons.com

Scalamandre
scalamandre.com

Schumacher
fschumacher.com

FLOORING & CARPETS

Beauvais Carpets
beauvaiscarpets.com

Doris Leslie Blau
dorisleslieblau.com

Madeline Weinrib
madelineweinrib.com

Merida Studio
meridastudio.com

Sam Kasten
samkasten.com

Shyam Ahuja
shyamahuja.com

Stark Carpet
starkcarpet.com

Vanderhurd
vanderhurd.com

Walking on Wood
walkingonwood.com

FURNITURE & LIGHTING

ABC Carpet & Home
abchome.com

Ann-Morris
ann-morris.com

Ballard Designs
ballarddesigns.com

B&B Italia
bebitalia.com/en

Chameleon Fine Lighting
chameleon59.com

Christian Astuguevieille

Christian Liaigre
christian-liaigre.us/en

Christopher Spitzmiller
christopherspitzmiller.com

Circa Lighting
circalighting.com

Design Within Reach
dwr.com

Espasso
espasso.com

Galerie des Lampes
galeriedeslampes.com

Harbour Outdoor
harbouroutdoor.com

Hinson Lighting
hinsonlighting.com

HB Home Design
hbhome.com

Hermes
usa.hermes.com

Holly Hunt
hollyhunt.com

Homenature
homenature.com

John Derian
johnderian.com

Jonathan Adler
jonathanadler.com

Just Scandinavian
justscandinavian.com

McGuire Furniture
mcguirefurniture.com

McKinnon and Harris
mckinnonharris.com

Mecox
mecox.com

Munder-Skiles
munder-skiles.com

Odegard
stephanieodegard.com

Philippe Anthonioz
philippe-anthonioz.com

Plexi-Craft
plexi-craft.com

Ralph Lauren
ralphlauren.com

Ralph Pucci
ralphpucci.net

Remains Lighting
remains.com

Restoration Hardware
restorationhardware.com

Robert Kime
robertkime.com

Robert Kuo
robertkuo.com

Rose Tarlow
rosetarlow.com

Serena & Lily
serenaandlily.com

Soane Britain
soane.co.uk

Solution
solution-co.com

Tucker Robbins
tuckerrobbins.com

Vaughan
vaughandesigns.com

Walter's Wicker
walterswicker.com

West Elm
westelm.com

PAINT

Benjamin Moore
benjaminmoore.com

Donald Kaufman Color
donaldkaufmancolor.com

Farrow & Ball
us.farrow-ball.com

Ralph Lauren Paint
ralphlaurenpaint.com

LANDSCAPE ARCHITECTS / RELATED

Buttercup Design Group
buttercupdesigngroup.com

Guido Toschi Marazzani Visconti
guidotoschi.it

Hollander Design Landscape Architects
hollanderdesign.com

LINENS & BATH ACCESSORIES

Casa Del Bianco
casadelbianco.com

E. Braun & Co.
ebraunnewyork.com

Haremlique
haremlique.com

Monogrammed Linen Shop
monogrammedlinenshop.com

Muriel Grateau

Waterworks
waterworks.com

ACKNOWLEDGMENTS

My gratitude to Dara Caponigro. I feel blessed by our special friendship. Thank you for taking time out of your busy life—on weekends and at the end of long days—to add your artistry, editorial eye, and vision to my book.

My thanks go to all the editors who believed in my work from the beginning and have allowed my interiors to grace their pages. Special thanks to Margaret Russell of *Architectural Digest* and Michael Boodro of *Elle Décor*, whose early and constant support means the world to a designer who works quietly and whose clients often do not want their houses published and wish to remain anonymous.

Thanks also to Clinton Smith and Carolyn Englefield at *Veranda* and Doretta Sperduto at *House Beautiful* for their support of my work.

To Amanda Teagle Essex, my collaborator, muse, and dear friend—and a true believer in my designs. The pursuit of beauty would not be the same without you.

My special thanks to Matthew Moneypenny, whose friendship I treasure. Matt, thank you for all your guidance and advice from the inception of this book.

With gratitude to my special friend Renee Harrison Drake who added her Midas touch to my introdiction.

Heartfelt thanks to Kathleen and Reha Kocatas for your friendship and for your help and support through the years.

To Martyn Lawrence-Bullard, thank you for believing in this book before it was a reality. I am so grateful to have you and the laughter we share in my life.

Thanks to my talented friend David Thomas of Solution Paris, who has always been generous in helping me with procuring and creating in the city of light.

To Mark Brockbank, thank you for your friendship and support and your meaningful presence in my life.

To my family: my parents, Barbara and Robert Whealon; my sister, Anne, and her husband, Michael Flanagan; my brother, Michael Whealon; and all my beautiful nieces and nephews—Ryan, Lainey, Malley, Hayes, and Step Flanagan and Teagan and Lily Whealon, who all have inspired me and made me see the world in different ways. To Annie: "a thing of beauty is a joy forever." I feel this way about our special bond—thank you for always being there for me—I love you!

With love and heartfelt thanks to my uncle Andrew Moquin for instilling in me the confidence to follow my dreams and helping them along the way during my studies with the Sotheby's Institute in London.

In memory of Kay Healy Moquin, my late aunt, an artist, a weaver, a graduate of Cranbrook Academy, and a decorator of some of the most beautiful houses in Grosse Pointe, Michigan. Thank you for opening my eyes to the arts and the world of design. Your spirit lives within me.

To my cousin Paul Healy—thank you for your friendship and business advice, and for introducing me to people and things outside of the design world that make my life richer, more interesting, and full of laughter with you at the helm.

Sincere thanks to my accountant, Jude Coard of Berdon LLP, and my financial advisor, Louise Armour of JP Morgan Chase.

To all the teachers and academics who play an integral part in the forming of young minds. My special thanks to the teachers who believed in and inspired me: Dr. Karen Edwards, Dr. Kimberly McMullen, and Dr. Judy Smith at Kenyon College; and Dr. Megan Aldrich at the Sotheby's Institute.

With thanks to Sue Wates, who opened her house in Pimlico to me when I was a student in London, and to the late artist Evelyn Smith, whose laughter filled 14 Moreton Terrace.

I have been fortunate to work with many exceptional people over the years at Timothy Whealon, Inc. I am grateful to each and every one of you for your invaluable contributions. An installation is never the same without Eric Bongartz on site.

My thanks to the talented architects I have collaborated with throughout the years—your work inspires and informs my own. Thank you also to the incredible craftsman, upholsterers, restorers, and artisans I have had the great pleasure of working with. I have so much respect for what you do, and collaborating with you has been one of the most joyous aspects of my career.

With appreciation for all the talented general contractors I have worked with around the globe. Special thanks to Keith Kirkpatrick of the I-Grace Company and Frank Cafone of Frank Cafone Construction.

Thank you to the amazing photographers who have captured my interiors with their artistry for their generosity of spirit in collaborating on this book, especially Melanie Acevedo, Jan Baldwin, Henry Bourne, Pieter Estersohn, Thibault Jeanson, Max Kim-Bee, Joshua McHugh, Tim Street-Porter, Simon Uptown, William Waldron, and Simon Watson. My thanks also to Olga Naiman, Carlos Mota, and Anita Sarsidi for adding their artistry and art direction on some of these shoots.

To Eugenia Santiesteban Soto, an oversized thank you for all your help on the photography for this book in all its various aspects.

Thank you to Charles Miers, publisher of Rizzoli International Publications, for his belief in this monograph of my work, as well as to Sandy Gilbert Freidus. With thanks and deep gratitude to my editor, Alexandra Tart, for her vision and patience, and for everything she did to make this book a beautiful reality.

To Doug Turshen, with thanks and heartfelt appreciation for your eye in creating a book that reflects the spirit of my designs, and to Dan Shaw for helping me capture the same in black ink. Thanks to Steve Turner for your patience and precision.

And, most important, thank you to my amazing clients, who have inspired my work with their personalities and whose collaborations have formed lasting friendships that I deeply treasure.

PHOTOGRAPHY CREDITS

Melanie Acevedo
www.melanieacevedo.com
Front cover, pages 89–113

Jan Baldwin, reprinted with permission of the publisher
© Ryland Peters & Small Ltd/Loupe Images/Jan Baldwin.
All rights reserved. pearsonlyle.co.uk/portfolio/jan_baldwin
page 13

Courtesy of Elle Décor
pages 139–49

Pieter Estersohn
www.pieterestersohn.com
pages 114–25, 167, 174–83, back cover

Thibault Jeanson
www.thibaultjeanson.photoshelter.com
page 165

Max Kim-Bee
www.maxkimbee.com
pages 2, 6, 14–27, 29–47, 49–67, 127–37, 206–11, 218–19

Joshua McHugh
www.joshuamchugh.com
pages 5, 162, 164, 169–73

Tim Street-Porter
www.timstreetporter.com
pages 153–61, 163

Simon Upton
www.simonupton.com
pages 187–201

William Waldron
www.williamwaldron.com
pages 9, 11, 203–04, 213–17, jacket flap portrait

Simon Watson
www.simonwatson.com
pages 68–87

First published in the United States of America in 2015
by Rizzoli International Publications, Inc.
300 Park Avenue South
New York, NY 10010
www.rizzoliusa.com

2015 2016 2017 2017 / 10 9 8 7 6 5 4 3 2 1

Distributed in the U.S. trade by Random House, New York

Designed by Doug Turshen with Steve Turner

Printed in China

ISBN-13: 978-0-8478-4333-6

Library of Congress Control Number: 2015934544